Vikings

Myths, Legends an

KIV Books

Copyright © 2017

Copyright © 2017 KIV Books

All rights reserved. This book or any portion thereof may not be reproduced or used in any manner whatsoever without the express written permission of the publisher except for the use of brief quotations in a book review.

Disclaimer

This book is designed to provide condensed information. It is not intended to reprint all the information that is otherwise available, but instead to complement, amplify and supplement other texts. You are urged to read all the available material, learn as much as possible and tailor the information to your individual needs.

Every effort has been made to make this book as complete and as accurate as possible. However, there may be mistakes, both typographical and in content. Therefore, this text should be used only as a general guide and not as the ultimate source of information. The purpose of this book is to educate.

The author or the publisher shall have neither liability nor responsibility to any person or entity regarding any loss or damage caused, or alleged to have been caused, directly or indirectly, by the information contained in this book.

Table of Contents

INTRODUCTION 5

THE HISTORY OF THE VIKINGS 7

VIKING MYTHOLOGY 15

VIKING LEGENDS 25

CONCLUSION 41

Introduction

Wildly swinging axes and swords upon majestic boats, Vikings have been a long-appreciated symbol of rage and power. They have been romanticized as overbearingly-manly warriors that plunder, loot and pillage villages all for the sake of dominance.

They've always been in modern media, but where did they come from? How did they start? What brought them to the apex of influence that still makes them relevant up to this day?

Their colorful history starts in the form of a migration. These warriors started out as nomads looking for new places to inhabit to prolong their lineage. Mainly travelling by sea, they've been defined as pirates that went from shore to shore, trading and occupying the villages that lived on the patches of land they would visit.

Said to have hailed from the countries of Sweden, Norway and Denmark, these seafaring people made their mark in the world from 700AD to 1100AD. That's more than 300 years of colorful and bloody history.

The earliest accounts of known Viking activity date all the way back to the 11th century in Lindisfarne, an island lying along the northern edges of England. From there, the northern origins of these warriors were sculpted.

This account wasn't a friendly one, though. The warriors were said to have looted and burned the church and other structures to the ground. Monks at that time were either killed or brought along as slaves when the Vikings were done with the area.

That point marked the beginning of years and years of attacks and loots under the Viking flags. Even the origin of their name comes from a derivation of the Scandinavian term for "pirate" which is "vikingr".

From that point, their influence spread all throughout Europe, cementing their names in the annals of scholars and monks during those times. While a large number of them pillaged and looted, other Vikings ended up as farmers and traders that settled in some of the lands they visited.

Their influence spread over the European lands like an epidemic, reaching all over the region, even reaching as far as Russia. They discovered the Americas long before the famed Columbus went on his expedition.

The History of the Vikings

"Never walk

Away from home

Ahead of your axe and sword.

You can't feel a battle in your bones

Or foresee a fight."

- The Book of Viking Wisdom

Pillaging their way into history, the Vikings have created a long saga of violence, wealth and trade within Europe. From the beginning of their violent conquests, the Vikings established their influence over the seas with their longships.

These ships, almost as iconic as the very men that rode them, were sturdy and large, capable of carrying many soldiers at one time. They were also designed to carry large loads of trade goods that the Vikings would use for their trade.

Their seafaring activities have led them to many lands, even all the way to North America. Upon reaching the new lands, the Vikings would choose to put up settlements in those areas and establish trade agreements with the original settlers in the area.

They were not just savages, though. They were also farmers that were looking for new lands to tame. Setting their own camps in the lands they visit, the Vikings introduced new forms of trade, religion and other cultural influences all throughout the world.

Viking Life

Similar to other cultures and lifestyles, Viking settlements had different castes. People were segregated into different classes which mostly dictated their daily lives.

At the bottom of the social structure were the Thralls. This level was composed mostly of slaves. These would be natives from the lands they conquered or traded from other Vikings. For the Vikings, slaves formed their primary source of hard labor.

Day to day chores as well as big construction efforts were done by slaves. Thralls were also used for farm work or where anywhere needed someone to get down and get dirty.

Usually, the children of a Thrall would also end up being slaves and had very little options if they desired to move up the social ranks. Despite their labor contributions, other Vikings looked down on the Thrall, giving them very little respect on account of their status.

They had no property and worked for other Vikings that were higher up the social ladder. These warriors would purposely raid some villages in order to replenish their supply of slaves. Some of the slaves would stay with the Viking settlers that would occupy the lands they would visit. Other slaves would be taken back to their homelands to serve the occupying Vikings that would head back to bring home their treasures and loot.

Above the Thralls were the Karls. In contrast to the status of slaves, the Karls were considered as "free peasants". They weren't considered as part of the aristocracy but they were capable of owning their own land, cattle and farms.

They didn't serve any lords and had to maintain the upkeep of their houses so that their families don't starve. In some cases, they also employ the services of Thralls so that they can till their lands and clean their estates.

Karls also did their share of manual labor. They were known to tend to their own farms, build their own houses as well as milking their own cows. Because of their status, they were allowed to devote their time to enriching their own estate.

Finally, the Jarls sat at the top of Viking life. They were the deemed aristocracy of the Viking race. They were the only ones deemed worthy to participate in politics and administration. They were also the ones that went on expeditions to explore new lands and acquire more wealth.

With their wealth, they were able to afford the largest estates and keep the most number of Thralls, animals and even horses. These nobles were occupied with helping their territories expand and find new places.

Excavations of Viking burial sites have also revealed that Jarls were buried with their property and their slaves. Their Thralls were killed along with their masters and buried together.

Interestingly, Viking women also enjoyed a few freedoms during their time. Evidence suggested that they could inherit property from others and become free peasants.

Viking Food

These Norsemen were lovers of meat. They had a deep appreciation of their meats and how to prepare them for various times of the day. The Vikings introduced various ways to cook their meats such as smoking, preserving and even curing meat.

With their seafaring nature, these warriors were also well-versed in handling various kinds of seafood. These items were prepared with soups, berries and even nuts to accompany their meals.

Of course, these Norse warriors were no strangers to the wonders of alcohol. They were great consumers of beer, wine and even mead. These drinks were consumed during their evening meals and festivals where they would gather and tell tales and sing songs.

Viking Warfare

Being a race of fierce warriors, the Vikings were especially adept at combat. For them, it wasn't just a matter of swinging swords and burning buildings. It was about besting their opponents and proving to the gods that they were superior in combat.

With the absence of laws against weapons, Viking men were free to carry their arms wherever they went. This allowed them to engage anyone in battle at their own leisure.

Depending on their wealth and status in the society, a Viking could be fully-clad in armor or could be just carrying a sheathed sword on their sides or back. The wealthiest of the lot were usually covered in armor, even to the point of wearing protective mail underneath their coverings.

Despite carrying swords with them all the time, Viking warfare consisted more of the usage of spears and axes. The Vikings followed in the example of Odin and Thor, believing in the effectiveness of more crude weapons.

This is the reason why more Viking warriors took to the charms of hand axes and battle hammers that could penetrate armor and shields. This allowed them to take out foes with a single strike, saving them energy and allowing them to take down more people whenever they would conduct raids.

Another interesting aspect of Viking warfare is their tendency to become enraged in combat. In such an enraged state, they would attack wildly as if disoriented. This goes against traditional warfare and thus made it difficult for their opponents to read their next action because of the unpredictability of their actions.

This is where the term berserkers came from. In order to produce this state, Viking warriors were known to ingest large amounts of beer or other hallucinogenic materials to pull of this feat.

Weaponry

The Vikings had a wide array of weapons to use in the middle of battle. One such example was the bow. Used for hunting and warfare, the bow was considered as an integral part of their arsenal.

Mainly used to start wars and raids, Viking bows were usually made of elm or ash wood. With their range reaching up to 20 meters. This allowed archers to cover a lot of ground before engaging their enemies with their blades.

Despite their use, Vikings considered the bow to be a mere complement to melee combat which was more honorable. A proud Viking warrior would rather fell an enemy within close range as a testament to their battle prowess.

In terms of close-ranged combat, the Vikings also favored the use of the spear. This was a more accessible weapon for the Karls that didn't have as much material and metal as the Jarls.

Used for both thrusting and throwing, the spear proved to be one of the most useful tools of warfare for the Vikings. One notable thing about their fighting style is the fact that they would hold spears with one hand, whether it be for throwing or thrusting.

The dependence of Vikings on spears can mainly be attributed to their chief god in Norse mythology. Odin the all-father was known to wield an almighty spear called Gugnir, which was known to never miss a mark when thrown.

On top of that, spears were easier to produce than swords as merely the tip needed to be created. In addition to this point, spears could be made with leftover metal and didn't need to be of the highest quality compared to the complex smith-work that swords required.

Besides swords, the Vikings would also wield a sword and shield combination. Despite popular opinion, Vikings would rarely use the sword. This was because this item was deemed more as a symbol of power than a tool of warfare.

It was only wealthy Vikings that could own a sword. These weapons were also made to be too big and unwieldy for battle. These weapons were adorned with gems and runes to express the wealth and status of whoever was wearing them.

These warriors also carried utility knives with them. These knives also served a dual purpose. Sometimes these small, concealed blades were used to skin animals and other hunting spoils. In battle, Vikings always rode into battle with knives on their persons.

If ever they were disarmed of their spear, armor and shield, they would take out their knives and force an even closer melee wherein they would forfeit their lives to take down their opponents with them.

Finally, there are the axes. Besides the spear, the axe would have been a major favorite among these warriors. With swords deemed as a luxury for a race of warriors that relished close-range combat, the axe was the best substitute. Since axes were designed to cut through lumber with a few blows, Vikings would be trained to punch holes in shields and armor with an axe.

The more trained warriors would even carry two axes on them instead of a shield as they felt more comfortable swinging two weapons in combat. Axes were also a better weapon for a berserker to wield.

The Decline of the Viking Age

Contrary to the pattern of other great empires, the Vikings were not occupied nor were they driven out of their lands. What happened was simply a shift in their lifestyle that also changed their identity as people.

This decline was seen at the rise of other Christian clans that were spreading their influence northward. Unconquered Christian churches and cities were now adapting to the raiding style of the Vikings.

Better defenses were made. More efficient warning systems were created and more effective weapons were crafted in response to their influence.

It was during the year 1066 that most scholars mark the end of the raids. At that point, there was only a small number of Viking aristocracy that had large amounts of wealth and land but there was an even larger number of slaves and free peasants that were more focused on enriching their own lands and settling down.

With this change in composition, the Vikings had less soldiers to train and more lands to till. When Christian kingdoms started training their soldiers to respond to their shock tactics and berserk fighting styles, raid attempts became less and less favorable as a means to acquire more wealth and land.

This development matured to the point that the Vikings considered raiding and pillaging a waste of time, money and labor. They now had found better ways to enrich themselves.

With this phenomenon, these people just started existing in their lands until they became part of the culture. The Vikings weren't called Vikings anymore but just regular citizens of the lands on which they lived.

Viking Mythology

"Moderately wise

A man should be

Not too crafty of clever.

A learned man's heart

Whose learning is deep

Seldom sings with joy"

- The Book of Viking Wisdom

One of the most prolific influences of Viking culture is their belief system. Their myths have given birth to some of the most iconic figures in the modern day. Their rich and colorful Norse stories and legends are still considered relevant and interesting even today.

The World Tree

According to these northerners, the world is not a planet orbiting the sun. It is a branch.

It is one of several branches that stem from the mother of all things: the world tree, known as Yggdrasil. This ash tree grows from something as the Well of Urd. Norsemen also refer to it as the well of destiny. This is the central image on which most of their religious stories are based.

The water from the well flows up to the tree, keeping it alive while the tress drops dewdrops from its leaves, back into the well in an endless cycle. This image also represents Norse belief on how the past influences the future and how sometimes, the present may also affect the past!

Within the Well of Destiny, three divine beings known as Norns reside. Their purpose it so inscribe the stories of everyone into Yggdrasil using runes. These three Norns are Verdandi, Urd and Skuld.

Interestingly, these names translate into the past, present and what will happen in Old Norse language. These ladies were said to hold more power and influence more than any other being that lay upon the many branches of the world tree.

The Worlds

Upon the branches of Yggdrasil rest the various lands for both gods, men and even beings of darkness.

Asgard

Perhaps the most popular and well-known of these lands is the realm of Norse gods and goddesses. Here, the gods wine, feast and go out on quests. They also bring in the souls of chosen warriors to live with them as demi-gods.

Midgard

This is known as the world of the mortals. Here, regular people (the Vikings) would spend their lives trying to get by, and proving themselves worthy of a place in Asgard. This is where the Vikings thought they lived.

Vaneheim

Unlike Greek mythology that has one pantheon of divinities, Norse mythology was home to two warring tribes. One of them was the Aesir, and the other, the Vanir.

If the Aesir resided in Asgard, the Vanir resided in Vaneheim. Although there are no sources that indicate which tribe is superior, the disputes between these tribes make up for many of the legends that are important parts of Viking mythology.

Joutenheim

If there were beings of divinity in Norse mythology, there would also be other fictional beings that went beyond the imagination. One such race were the giants. Naturally larger than people and even gods, they resided in the forests of Joutenheim.

Alfheim

There were also elves in Norse mythology. They resided in the land of Alfheim, keeping to themselves but occasionally making contact with humans and gods alike. Known to be very graceful beings that emitted light from themselves, they have been considered as demi-gods in their own regard.

Niflheim

On a more interesting note, there are also lands that have eternal weathers.. Niflheim is such a place; but it has very important bearings in the creation of things.

Niflheim was known as the land of eternal darkness and ice. It was wear the ice giants lived. These were magical beings that utilized the powers of cold. Take note that this wasn't the recreation of the underworld. It was simply devoid of light and was always snowing. It had nothing to do with evil.

Perhaps the most significant aspect of Niflheim was the fact that it's separation from its counterpart brought about the first being to walk among the branches of Yggdrasil.

Muspelheim

If there was a land of eternal cold, then it would also make sense that there is a land of eternal heat as well. This is where Muspelheim comes in. Considered as the land of the fire giants, it was always bright and hot.

Svartalfheim

If elves were already present in Norse mythology, then dwarves are close by. These stout and sturdy smiths lived underneath the ground and the mountains in the land of Svartalfheim.

Considered as master smiths and craftsmen, their services were usually required by the Aesir and Vanir to create various items for them. One very iconic item of their creation was Thor's hammer, Mjollnir. It was said to have been created within the heart of a dying star, giving the hammer its magnificent powers.

Hel

Deemed as the Norse underworld, this is where the souls of the dead go. If they haven't been called to Asgard to serve the gods, the departed make their way to hel to live out the afterlife.

Interestingly, popular notions of the afterlife were different during Viking times. For these norsemen, Hel isn't a pace of eternal suffering. In fact, it's just a continuation of life. It's another stage of existing. There aren't any pyres and volcanoes and agonizing activities like the underworld of Greek mythology and even Christianity.

With that in mind, it can be said that Vikings had a different view of life after death.

The Aesir

Probably the most prolific and popular in modern culture, the Aesir were considered the divine equivalent of Greek gods and goddesses. Just like their format as well, the Aesir were gods assigned to various aspects and virtues in daily life.

These Aesir rested upon the world known as Asgard, and were thus referred to as Asgardians. Each of them having their own history and stories that celebrate their life and accomplishments.

Odin

Considered as the equivalent of Zeus in Greek mythology, Odin was considered the "all-father" for the malevolent beings that resided within Asgard. He sat on a pedestal above all the other Asgardians and enjoyed a seat at his throne in Valhalla.

Valhalla was considered to be the equivalent of mount Olympus, dwelling place of the gods. In Valhalla, though, human warriors that have shown promise and valor in combat are rewarded a place in this hall upon their death on the battlefield. There, they would feast and do battle for the rest of their lives.

Odin is portrayed as a long-bearded man wielding a large, terrifying spear known as Gugnir. This weapon of legend was known to have never missed a target.

Odin also had the fastest horse in all of the land, for it had eight legs. This steed was called Sleipnir. On his steed and with his spear in hand, Odin would go on adventures all around Yggdrasil, visiting the various lands and learning new things.

This is probably the reason why he is more fondly known as the god of wisdom. He was pictured to be a wise man, seeking to increase his knowledge by travelling.

In fact, his thirst for wisdom has brought him some grave experiences. In most literature and paintings, it is seen that he wears an eye patch over one eye. This wasn't a war accident or a duel. Odin paid an eye to be able to drink from the very Well of Urd at the bottom of Yggdrasil.

Staying true to his desire for knowledge, Odin created two ravens to serve him. Each day, these ravens would circle the various worlds perched on Yggdrasil and watch everything exist. At the end of the day, the ravens would come back to Odin and tell him of the things they have learned.

Thor

Known as the god of thunder, he enjoys reign as the son of Odin. To control lightning, he wields the magical hammer known as Mjollnir, which was bestowed to him by Odin.

Thor was known to have been adept at slaying giants, another race perched somewhere else on Yggdrasil. This talent made him the focus of many songs and poems about battle and death. His adventures and conquests using his hammer have also been accompanied by a magic gauntlet that he wears that increases his strength.

Loki

Considered as one of the most interesting characters within the pantheon of Norse mythology, Loki was considered the apex of mischief and deceit.

His antics have gotten him into great danger, even jeopardizing the situations of other gods and goddesses. His ability to change form into other people and even animals allows him to trick others to get his way.

Interestingly, Loki isn't a full god, being born from a giant and a goddess. This means he was a product of two warring factions within Yggdrasil. Because of that, many stories have depicted him deceiving and helping both sides from time to time. This series of actions has made him a popular topic of debate among scholars.

There have been many arguments regarding his origin, purpose, allegiance and even his gender. One of the more interesting stories involving Loki was him giving birth to Sleipnir, Odin's steed. He did this by turning himself into a mare and mating with another horse.

Baldur

Another popular entity within Asgard was Baldur. Being the brother of Thor, he was born from the union of Odin and Frigg. He was very handsome and liked by all.

In fact, his story was one of the more interesting tales in Norse mythology. It started with him dreaming of his death. When he told his mother Frigg about his premonitions, Frigg started travelling all over the world to save her son.

She did this by asking everything and everyone to make an oath that they would not harm Baldur. After getting almost everything to take an oath, the gods proved Frigg's efforts by trying to throw things at Baldur. They threw axes, spears, swords and anything else they could find. All of it just bounced off or just flew right over his head.

At that point, Loki took to his mischief and asked Frigg if there was anything she overlooked on her quest to protect Baldur. She said she did not ask the small mistletoe to make an oath, with it being such a small and harmless thing.

With that information, Loki had a spear of mistletoe made and asked another god to throw it at Baldur for sport. Without the oath, the spear hit Baldur and ultimately killed him.

Frigg

If Odin was the father-figure in Asgard, she would have ultimately been the mother-figure, being his female partner. Considered as the goddess of beauty and marriage, she gave birth to Baldur, one of the most endearing personas of Norse myths.

Stories depict her being driven by a chariot pulled by cats, giving her blessings to weddings and childbirths.

Interestingly, other accounts say that she had loose morals because of her estate as high-goddess in Valhalla. She was known to have had sexual conquests and liaisons with other beings.

Tyr

Known as the god of war, Tyr was a famous diety among the Vikings with their plundering ways. Warriors would ask for his blessing upon reaching new lands, hoping to engage in battle and test their skills and luck.

On top of being the god of war, Tyr was also closely associated with law and justice. He was known as the bearer of truth and meted out punishment to those that made infractions to the laws at that time.

Asgard was home to not just these beings, but many more divinities that ruled over the lands. Each of them have their own stories, songs and poems that depict their adventures and sacrifices and feats of legend. The Vikings call upon these stories as they lived, making it part of their culture and lifestyle.

The Vanir

Not to be confused with evil forces, the Vanir were another gathering of divinities on another branch of Yggdrasil. They had their own land as well as their own corresponding problems and adventures.

Compared to the Aesir, the Vanir were more attuned with the use of magic. They were sorcerers and mages that had great knowledge and wisdom. Although they were pictured as waging wars against the Aesir, they most certainly were not evil by nature.

Among the Vanir, the most prominent are Freya and Njord. These divinities were closely associated with fertility and happiness, which made them play a vital part during the warring stage of the two tribes.

The Aesir - Vanir War

Being a talented magician, Freya was known for her proficiency in the art of Seidr. This practice concerned changing ones' destiny, health and even wealth. This talent made her quite popular among the worlds, even in Asgard.

When Freyas' travels brought her to the land of the Aesir, the gods were immediately drawn to her talents, calling on her to fix most of their problems. Being able to lift curses, cure disease and change fate, she was quite the commodity.

Unfortunately, the Aesir's dependence on Freya mutated into a realization that they were setting aside their morals and loyalty for a sorceress that was not even a part of their tribe.

With that notion in mind, the Aesir branded Freya as an evil witch and burned her three times in an attempt to end her sorcery. Interestingly, Freya always came back from the ashes after being burnt.

It was this act that started the hatred between the Aesir and the Vanir, with each side claiming a debt owed by the other tribe. Eventually, this hatred blossomed into a war that lasted years.

After countless encounters and exchanges of upper hands, both tribes could not seem to overpower the other. It was this realization that they decided to hold a truce.

In order to solidify this truce, both tribes decided to offer the opponent a hostage or "guest"; which was one of their own kind to live on the other side. The Aesir surrendered Mimir and Hoenir, both wise and knowledgeable. The Vanir gave up Freya, her brother Freyr and their mother Njord.

This is why despite being originally Vanir at heart, Freya ended up in most tales as seated within Valhalla in Asgard, assisting Odin on various matters.

Ragnarok

One very interesting facet of Viking mythology is the premise of the end of all things, which also turns out to be a cyclic transition into a new beginning. This is the purpose of Ragnarok, or a fabled war that will lead to the end of the gods.

Roughly translating to "the twilight of the gods", Ragnarok refers to a series of events that cannot be stopped, which will bring about the end of the worlds on Yggdrasil.

Prophecies have foretold that a great war between gods and giants will descend upon Asgard, with each god falling to a specific encounter. Even the all-powerful Odin will meet his match at Ragnarok. The ice and fire giants will descend upon Asgard and destroy everything. The fire giant known as Surt will turn everything to ash.

From this destruction, a new world will arise from the unions of the land of ice and the land of fire once again.

This gives insight into how the Vikings looked at life. For them, there is just a continuous journey from one state to the next. For them, their lives are already written down, just waiting to happen and end.

Viking Legends

"Wake early

If you want

Another man's life or land

No lamb

For the lazy wolf.

No battles won in bed."

- The Viking Book of Wisdom

Besides the stories mentioned in the previous chapter, the Vikings had many other stories of which they sung over ale and successful raids. Given their combative nature, most of their favorite legends entail brave and skillful heroes taking on some of the most dangerous missions.

Beowulf

Perhaps the most popular epic among all Norse legends, the poem of Beowulf tells the tale of this warrior throughout the ages.

Originally a hero of the land of Geats, Beowulf's adventure started out on a visit to Scandinavia. Where the king of Danes enlisted his help to defeat a monster that has raided his halls; the Grendel.

Similar to bigfoot, Grendel was pictured as a giant, hair-covered monster that feasted on men and could tear limbs apart. The name Grendel was enough to strike fear in the hearts of men, except Beowulf.

Upon arriving at the hall, Beowulf and his men prepare in the mead-hall for the attack of the beast. Just outside, Grendel was stalking her new prey, sizing them up as it prepared to attack.

As Beowulf and his party were asleep, Grendel burst through the front entrance, startling the team. It grabbed the first soldier closest and devoured him right away. The poem was specific about this feat and gave full details.

Upon approaching the second solider to eat, the Grendel was surprised to see that this soldier fought back at broke its grip. This second soldier was none other than Beowulf. What followed after this was a great battle.

With only few soldiers to help him, Beowulf engaged Grendel in a spectacular melee. This encounter ended with Beowulf ripping off the arm of the beast. This caused Grendel to flee back to where it came, where it died of its wounds.

But this isn't where the story ends, for Grendel was but an offspring of its mother, who was devastated at Grendel's death. Driven by revenge, the mother attacks the mead-hall where Beowulf and his party waited, giving Beowulf the idea to attack the monster's den to finish off the beasts.

What transpired at the cave was another epic battle. There, the mother was able to disarm Beowulf and was about to deliver the finishing blow to the hero. Fortunately, Beowulf caught sight of an antique sword in the cave, probably from another slain adventurer. With that blade in hand, Beowulf was able to defeat the mother of Grendel, ridding the king of Danes of this problem.

To bring proof, Beowulf found the corpse of Grendel and took its head as a souvenir. Upon showing his spoils to the kind, he was heavily rewarded for his feat of bravery.

Upon returning to Geat, word of his victory against the Grendel had already reached his hometown. Because of that, he was gifted with the crown of the land and became ruler. But the story does not end there.

50 years after his victory against Grendel, king Beowulf faced one more challenge. One of Beowulf's' slaves earned the audacity to steal a goblet from the den of a dragon that was sleeping in its lair not far from his kingdom. Upon finding the goblet stolen, the dragon goes on a rampage, burning everything in sight.

Weary of the attack, Beowulf sets out to quell the beast and asks his guards to allow him to fight the beast alone. Upon encountering the dragon, Beowulf finds that he is at a disadvantage.

Upon seeing this, one of Beowulf's' soldiers by the name of Wiglaf comes to his aid. With the odds evened-out, the pair was eventually able to defeat the dragon. Unfortunately, Beowulf had already been mortally wounded during this battle.

Upon his death, Beowulf is cremated and mourned over by his soldiers and people. Without their king and bravest warrior, they were at the mercy of the other invading tribes.

The Legend of Creation

The Vikings believed that the first ever being was a giant that sprung forth from a union of extreme heat and cold at the beginning of all things. This beginning was called Ginnungagap.

This was known as a big, dark abyss from which everything started. There were no lands, people, gods and even giants. There were only two things that were present at the edges of this darkness: the heat of Muspelheim and the cold of Niflheim.

The interaction of the heat and the ice bore the first being to ever walk upon the branches of Yggdrasil; the giant known as Ymir. He was born from ice drops from Niflheim that were melted by the fires of Muspelheim.

Interestingly, Ymir was gifted with the capacity to reproduce on his own. This allowed him to create more giants when he would sweat. These giants increased in number and thus, the first race on Yggdrasil was born.

But the creation did not stop there. As Ymir's race was growing in number, the ice from Niflheim was still melting, giving birth to another being. This time, it was a large cow that was called Audhumbla.

Now, Ymir was able to nourish himself and his people with the milk from this cow. In turn, the cow was able to lick the ice, nourishing itself from the salt-licks. This caused further melting from the ice.

With more melting, another being was found from the ice. It was neither giant nor cow. This time, it was the first god; Buri. He would be the very first member of the Aesir tribe.

The god Buri had a son, called Bor. This god then married another giant named Bestla, the daughter of another giant Bolthorn. The union of this god and giant gave birth to another member of the Aesir, Odin. Bor had two other sons, Vili and Ve, who then became Odin's brothers.

This band of brothers pulled together to plot the downfall of Ymir, the first giant to create the rest of the world. After killing Ymir, Odin and his brothers created the rest of the world from the remains of Ymir.

From the blood of Ymir, they created the seas and the oceans. From the skin and muscles, the land. Fruits, vegetables and other plants were created from his hair. The sky and the heavens were formed from his skull and his brain. Thus began the other realms that rested upon Yggdrasil.

After the creation of the world and everything in it, Odin and the other gods fashioned the first people. They were called Ask and Embla. They were crafted from the trunks of two trees and the land in which they were created was fenced off. This was how Midgard was created. The fence that Odin and his brothers created protected the land from the giants.

From this story, it could be said that the Vikings believed that something must die for something else to be born; just as the world was created from the remains of a giant. This led them to believe that they were creating something new when they invaded other areas and burned everything down to the ground.

The Mead of Poetry

Thought of as one of the longer and older stories in Norse mythology, this tale describes the origins of poets and singers and scholars with their natural talent for reason.

At the end of the war between the Aesir and the Vanir, both tribes agreed to a truce. This was when they handed over a select number of their own tribe to live amongst the other as an honored guest.

Despite this trade, the Vanir thought that they had gotten the short end of the bargain. They beheaded their Aesir guest and sent the head back to Odin. This started another upset in the balance, leading the two forces back to war.

It was after another stalemate that the two tribes went into another truce. This time, instead of exchanging hostages once more, they solidified their agreement by having their heads spit into a cauldron to symbolize their unity.

This act gave birth to a new human, Kvasir. Having been born of this unusual truce between two warring tribes of divinities, he was gifted with incredible wisdom. There was no issue he could not resolve on his own.

With this gift, Kvasir travelled the different realms, sharing his gift as he met new beings and gods.

Sadly, Kvasir met his demise when he came upon two dwarves named Galar and Fjalar. This pair was known for their murderous affairs. Having found a victim with Kvasir, the pair killed the creation of the gods and turned his remains into a mead.

What resulted was a magical substance that could turn anyone that drank it into a poet or scholar of the highest caliber. They hid the mead and formulated an excuse for the gods about what happened to Kvasir.

When they were eventually questioned about what happened to the scholar, the dwarves merely retorted that Kvasir suffocated out of his own knowledge. His greatest gift became his greatest weakness as well.

After having gone scoff-free for the murder of Kvasir, the duo changed their sights to a giant this time, by the name of Gilling. The dwarves invited the giant out to sea with them where they drowned him just for fun.

Distraught, Gilling's wife mourned over the death of her husband, earning her the ire of his murderers. This cause the dwarves to kill her as well by dropping a large stone on her head to silence her weeping.

This additional crime earned the dwarves the vengeance of Gilling's son, Suttung. He hunted the dwarves and tied them down at sea during low tide. Upon the coming of the tide, the waves would drown the dwarves as well.

Fearing for their lives, the dwarves asked for mercy. Having knowledge of the mead, Sutting struck a bargain with the dwarves. He would let them go if they surrendered the mead to him.

Upon claiming the mead, Sutting hid the mead which were in vats underneath a large mountain. Upon storing the vats, the ordered his daughter Gunnlod to guard the mead for him.

Having learned of the location of the mead, Odin sat restless in his throne, desiring the abilities provided by the mead. He then began his conquest to obtain a sample for himself. He journeyed down to the land of the giants in search of the mountain.

His quest brought him to Suttung's brother Baugi, who had farmlands that were tended to by nine farmhands. To get into the estate, Odin changed his form into that of another farmhand and approached the nine workers, offering to sharpen their sickles for them.

Using a special whetstone, Odin sharpened the sickles of the workers to such an extent that the farmhands desired to buy the whetstone from Odin. Upon getting the interest of the farmhands, Odin agreed to give them the tool for a dear price.

He hurled the stone into the air, allowing the farmhands to catch the whetstone as it plummeted to the ground. Sadly, the workers ran into each other with their sharp sickles in hand. This killed the helpers all in one fell swoop.

Seizing the opportunity, Odin offered his services to Baugi who was suddenly bereft of nine farmhands. Odin's bargain was simple; in exchange for access to the mead, Odin would do the work of nine farmhands for Baugi.

Baugi confronted the offer and said that he had no influence over who gets the mead for Suttung had it guarded even against his own brother; but seeing such a good offer, Baugi offered a different proposal. Should Odin perform the work of nine people, he would help the disguised god gain access to the mead.

The giant and the worker had a deal. Upon completion of his end of the bargain, Odin awaited Baugi to fulfill his end. Baugi accompanied the disguised god to his brother to explain their deal in hopes that Suttung would share some of this mead. Surprisingly, Suttung had no interest in sharing the mead with his brother nor his strange friend.

Upon that rejection, Odin and Baugi ventured to the back of the mountain at the area closest to the base where the mead was hidden. There, Odin provided and auger for the giant to use. The plan now was to drill a hole into the chamber to get access to the mead.

Once the hole had been drilled, Odin quickly changed form, revealing his deceit. He turned into a snake and slithered through the hole that Baugi had made. The giant tried to stab the creature but the shapeshifting all-father got in unscathed.

Upon getting into the base of the mountain, Odin travelled to the lair where the mead was guarded. Before meeting Gunnlod, Odin turned himself into a young man to entice the female giant.

Upon meeting Gunnlod, Odin's plan had worked and he won the giant's favor. She agreed to give him three sips of the mead in exchange for three nights with the form in which Odin took.

With his goal close at hand, Odin agreed to sleep with the giant for three days in exchange for a sip of the mead. After the third night of sleeping with the giant, Odin gained access to the vats that stored the mead.

Despite their agreement only being sips of the mead, Odin emptied all the content of the vats in on go. Shocked, Gunnlod realized Odin's deception but it was too late. Odin had taken all the mead and was ready to escape.

Changing shape one more time, Odin became an eagle and flew out of the chamber and into the sky with his head towards Asgard. Enraged, Gunnlod informed her father of the theft. Suttung, unyielding to the crime at hand, also put his magic to use and turned into another eagle as well and pursued Odin as he flew.

On Asgard, the other gods saw Odin approach in his eagle form and noticed that he was being followed by Suttung. The gods prepared to protect their lord by forming a perimeter around Asgard. As soon as Odin had reached his land, Suttung could no longer follow. Upon giving up, he returned in anguish.

Triumphant in his quest, Odin returned with all the mead in his throat. As he was about to transfer the mead into a container of his own, a few drops of the mead fell from his beak and onto Midgard. This is why there are poets and scholars within the realm of man. Although those are just mediocre and deplorable artisans. Odin saves the best mead for those he deems worthy to inherit the mead's powers.

The Building of the Asgard Walls

Before Asgard was known to be the impregnable fortress it was, it was merely a land where the gods lived. They had no form of defense against other tribes and beings that wanted to take over.

Seeing this situation, a giant offered his services to gods. This giant smith promised the Aesir that he would build them an impregnable wall that will protect Asgard.

In exchange for building the wall, the giant had a simple condition. He wanted to marry the goddess Freya and obtain the sun and the moon in return for his services.

Finding the terms unbelievable, the Aesir banded together and thought of a way to get the giant to build them the wall without sacrificing the goddess Freya nor the sun and moon. The premise of having a guard wall was attractive to them but the price seemed too steep.

As they deliberated their choices, the trickster Loki came up with a seemingly grand idea. He suggested that the Aesir agree to the price of the giant but change some other stipulations.

The Aesir will grant the giant Freya and the moon and the sun on the condition that he finishes the wall within just one winter without any help except from that of the giant's horse.

Surprisingly, the giant agreed and started to work. To the shock of the Aesir, the giant was very capable of working within their time frame. With the help of his horse, Svadilfari, the giant was able to do the work of multiple men, coming close to completion nearing the end of the winter.

This caught the gods off-guard. If the giant was to complete his task, they would have to fill their end of the bargain and give up the night sky and the morning sun, along with the goddess Freya.

Frustrated, the Aesir bound Loki, who instigated the idea that they could dupe the giant into working for free. The gods promised to kill Loki if he did not find a way out of this conundrum.

Fearing for his life, Loki pledged that he would find a way to stop the giant and his steed. Interestingly, most of the work was done by the steed instead of the giant. The horse was doing twice the amount of work that the giant was doing. It was through there that Loki found his opening.

Transforming himself into a beautiful mare, Loki showed himself to the horse Svadilfari, enticing the beast. His plan succeeded. Instead of working towards the wall, the horse ran after Loki. He led the horse away from the giant with mere days away from the end of the winter.

Distraught, the giant could not finish his end of the bargain, but had already put in a substantial amount of work that the unfinished product was already an impregnable fort for the gods even without the finishing touches.

But a deal was a deal. The giant had failed to finish the wall. His payment was an excruciating death at the hands of Thor and Mjollnir. A blow to the giant's head shattered his crown into smaller pieces, never to be put together.

As for Loki, he was eventually found by Svadilfari. There, they mated as was the steed's desire. From that union, Loki the mare gave birth to one of the most iconic images in Norse mythology; the steed Slepinir. It had eight legs and was the swiftest horse of all which eventually become property of Odin.

The Ring of Andvari

This story is considered a favorite among the Vikings for it entails much gold, adventure, deception and glorious battle.

On one occasion, Odin, Loki, and Hoenir ventured towards the land of the dwarves. Along their way, they came across an otter. Figuring the skin of the otter was ideal for a souvenir, Loki killed the otter while the other two gods skinned the animal.

Upon arriving at the land of the dwarves, the three Aesir met with the dwarf king, Odin bragged about a bagskin made from the otter they had murdered along the way. To the shock of the dwarf king, the skin of the otter happened to belong to none other than his very own son!

Filled with rage, the dwarf king ordered for the capture of the gods and held them accountable for the murder of his son who could change form into an otter. Along with his two remaining sons Fafnir and Regin, the dwarf king Hriedmar seized Odin and his party.

In order to save his lords, Loki was set free to come back with ransom to bail out Odin from captivity. As per dwarf customs, Loki had to fill the bagskin with enough gold to fill it. It was a tall order but Loki knew where he was going to find that much gold.

That gold was going to come from a dwarf that went by the name Andvari. Being a solitary dwarf, he lived alone underneath a waterfall. Gifted with the power to turn into a fish, he was able to live with nature and feed off the land.

Andvari had a very special treasure; a ring. This trinket allowed him to turn anything into gold. For a dwarf living alone, that allowed him that helped him amass a great amount of gold with little effort. He hoarded gold in his dwelling thanks to this ring.

With that information, Loki began preparing his approach to obtain that ring and all of Andvari's gold. With the help of a magical net, Loki turned himself into a spear and caught the fish-dwarf at the waterfall.

Held captive, Andvari pleaded for his freedom. With not much else to barter, Andvari had to give up his ring and his gold to Loki, who was in dire need of a large amount of gold.

But this exchange was not without revenge. Angered by Loki's trickery, Andvari placed a curse on his ring and his gold. Anyone who would own his gold and ring would immediately experience great misfortune and downfall.

With the curse being intended for Loki, the gold was secured by the trickster god. Loki happily took the gold and the ring, knowing that it wasn't going to end up with him.

With the gold in hand, he presented the spoils to the dwarf king who was satisfied with the tribute. Odin's party was set free and the gods were off on their way once again.

With the treasure in the dwarf's possession, Andvari's curse immediately took effect. The jealousy and the greed immediately took possession of Fafnir, the dwarf prince. The greed had driven Fafnir to murder his own father to obtain the ring and the gold.

Upon the realization of his plans, Fanfir horded the gold and locked himself away to guard it. He even denied his own brother his fair share of the treasure. With the curse of the gold steadily coming to fruition, Fafnir slowly turned into a senseless dragon.

Seeking Retribution, Regin plots to destroy his dragon brother and stop the curse of the gold. He seeks the help of a warrior who went by the name of Sigurd. In order to defeat the dragon, the two allies sharpen their fangs and prepare their attack.

In order to defeat such a dragon, Regin crafted a special sword for the warrior Sigurd. In exchange for helping the warrior engage the dragon, Regin wanted a portion of the gold and the very heart of the dragon Fafnir.

Sigurd agrees to the conditions and together, they bring down Fafnir and gain access to his treasures. But before falling to Sigurd, Fafnir uttered a warning that he whoever owns the treasure shall have nothing but bad luck.

Sigurd then claimed that he would not touch this treasure, claiming that it was the nature of all men to die and he did not fear death at all. With that, he claimed the title of Dragonslayer with his legendary blade called Gram.

In the process of preparing the heart of the dragon, Sigurd accidentally burns his finger and drink a few drops of dragon blood. With that, Sigurd gained the ability to understand and talk to birds.

It was through this gift that Sigurd learned from some birds that Regin was plotting to finish off Sigurd to claim all the gold to himself. The birds spoke of Regin's intention of thrusting Sigurd from behind as they feasted on the heart of the dragon Fafnir.

Using the very sword Regin made, Sigurd beats Regin to his scheme by killing the dwarf first and obtaining all the treasure to himself in the process. The hero cleaved the head off the deceptive dwarf.

Besides the betrayal of Regin, the birds also spoke of a maiden that would make a great conquest for Sigurd. The birds sang of the maiden Brynhildr that lay sleeping within a castle that was surrounded by a terrible ring of red fire.

So Sigurd rode straight to this castle after vanquishing the dwarf brother Fafnir and Regin. The myths he heard were not lying. There was a castle enveloped in flames. It was then he knew that there would be a sleeping maiden inside the castle, waiting for a knight to brave the fire and wake her up.

So Sigurd rode his horse through the fire. His trusty steed leapt through the flames and into the castle where his prize was waiting. There, he woke up the maiden Brynhildr, who was wearing a shield like a warrior.

As it turns out Brynhildr was a Valkyrie, battle maidens that assisted Odin in choosing heroes from Midgard to live and do battle in Valhalla. Brynhildr was cursed by Odin to sleep in the castle until a worthy warrior would brave the ring of fire and wake her from her slumber.

With the maiden as his prize, Sigurd rode away to his next adventure into the ring's curse, which have gave as a gift to Brynhildr.

Sigurd then met a king with a beautiful daughter and a witch queen. The daughter, Gudrun, fell in love with Sigurd almost immediately and was devastated at the fact that Sigurd loved Brynhildr the battlemaiden.

Determined to please Gudrun, the queen plotted to separate the hero and the Valkyrie. She created a forgetfulness potion and put it in Sigurd's drink. Upon drinking, Sigurd forgot all about his love for Brynhildr and fell in love with Gudrun.

The deception of the queen did not end there. Having a son by the name of Gunnar, the queen asked Sigurd to ride with Gunnar to woo Brynhildr, whom Sigurd left at their castle surrounded by a ring of fire.

Saddened by Sigurd's betrayal, Brynhildr lay in their castle, unwilling to accept any suitors. She had but one condition; that she would only marry he who would brave the ring of fire around her castle.

Gunnar tried his best to leap through the flames but his horse was unfit for the task. Knowing that Sigurd was the only one who could do this, Gunnar used magic of his own to change his shape into that of Sigurd and Sigurd into that of his shape.

Sigurd, shaped as Gunnar, rode through the flames and into the tower, fulfilling Brynhildr's challenge. Thinking that Sigurd was Gunnar, Brynhildr had no choice but to fulfill her promise and marry Gunnar. She returned the cursed ring to Sigurd who was still in Gunnar's form.

After claiming Brynhildr, Gunnar used magic once more to return to his original form and did the same to Sigurd. Gunnar married Brynhildr and Sigurd came back to Gudrun, to whom he now gave the cursed ring of Andvari.

During Gunnar's wedding the witch's magic potion of forgetfulness wore off and Sigurd remembered everything. He remembered that he loved Brynhildr and was tricked by the queen. Seeing that Brynhildr had already married Gunnar, Sigurd kept silent so as not to scandalize the affair.

During the length of their marriage, Gudrun and Brynhildr went for a bath in the lake together. Brynhildr, being a Valkyrie, waded into the deepest part of the lake to show Gudrun that she and Gunnar were superior because Gunnar was able to cross the flames of her tower for her.

Enraged at the gesture, Gudrun slipped and revealed Gunnar's secret to Brynhildr. She told the Valkyrie that Gunnar changed Sigurd into his shape to brave her tower for him. This story devastated the Valkyrie's honor as she was deceived and was married to a dishonest man.

Upon hearing her plight, Sigurd came to comfort Brynhildr and speak to her on the matter. Sadly, Sigurd was met with bitterness and anger. Wishing for Sigurd to die, Brynhildr told Sigurd that it was too late for her to be happy for her honor had been broken.

Plotting the death of her former lover, Brynhildr prepared a maddening potion made of snake poison and the meat of a wolf. She fed this poison Gunnar's younger brother who was immediately overcome with murderous intent.

Storming into Sigurd's room, the man stabbed the hero and pinned him to the bed. Just before he died, Sigurd grabbed his fabled sword and threw it at his murderer, slicing him in half.

Gudrun mourned her husband's death. This was followed by Brynhildr's laughter over the success of her revenge. Stricken by grief, even Sigurd's famed horse died of sadness. In the midst of all the madness, Brynhildr also fell weeping until her poor heart gave out, leaving her lifeless.

Thus, Sigurd was clad in his golden armor and laid on a boat to be burned at sea. On that boat they also laid his horse Grani and his true love, Brynhildr. The boat burned in the middle of sea, bringing it's dead passengers to the bottom where the curse of the ring had finally been fulfilled.

Conclusion

Despite their bloody history, the Vikings have made their way into the minds and imaginations of artisans in today's day and age. Their violence and rage has become the content of many popular stories and epics that have stood the test of time.

Despite the popular notion, one important thing to remember about them was that they were people that were trying to maintain their lifestyle in a very perilous time. Religions were just starting to form their grips in the minds and hearts of people. Only the strongest were sure to survive; and survive they did.

They weren't savages as popular media would portray them. They were a civilized race that had their own laws and rules to ensure the propagation of their way of life.

They also weren't just warriors. They were farmers, poets, scholars, shamans, politicians and students. Pillaging and raiding was just a small part of their culture. They were a merry-making bunch that also had their own share of challenges.

As a final tidbit, forego any notion that the Vikings were unkempt warriors that wore horned helmets. Much historical evidence points out to normally designed helmets that had no horns. Their helmets had metal frames and were covered in animal skins or other metals to protect their heads.

On top of that, excavated Viking relics prove that they took pride in their appearances. They had combs and brushes with which to fix their hair and beards.

Hopefully this short book has helped you to increase your curiosity about Vikings even more. If so, then keep searching and learning, there's always so much more you can learn and explore. Thank You for reading and good luck.

Printed in Great Britain
by Amazon